The Boy in the Striped

About the book

The Boy in the Striped Pyjamas is already a modern classic. Its story of a young boy caught up in the realities of war make it one of the essential reads for children learning about the Second World War and its impact on children's lives. Its combination of fiction placed within historical fact make it ideal for Year 6 and the transition to Year 7. It could be studied as a serialised class novel and there are links with many literary genres – it has an historical setting, it places an emphasis on one viewpoint and it raises issues and dilemmas.

The book has two levels. Its most basic level is the simple story of a nine-year-old boy (Bruno) who is baffled by sudden upheaval from his comfortable home in a bustling city environment to an empty desolate area with no school or friends. His confusion is increased by what he hears and sees around him, in particular the people in striped pyjamas and the fence. Lonely and struggling to hold on to memories of his previous happy life, Bruno tries to occupy himself with former pleasures: exploration and play. He makes his adventurous journey to the baffling fence, and there finds a much longed-for friend. He finally gets his wish to visit his new friend on the other side of the fence. In so doing, he begins the final part of his journey.

Bruno's innocent view of life, his journey and his friendship across a fence form the spine of the story. They emphasise the innocence of childhood, the simplicity of easy solutions and the cruelty of unnecessary division. This light fictional world contrasts with the dark historical context.

The author creates a more complex level to the story by making implicit references. The reader has to piece together casual descriptions, small incidents and unexplained behaviour. The truth about Bruno's new home and final journey are never stated. Yet the horrific facts are all the more powerful for being implicit.

The author has broached a frightening subject. The genocide of the Second World War may seem a subject too monstrous for a new generation to confront, yet there are powerful arguments that it must not be forgotten. This story, with its deceptive simplicity, helps the young reader to confront this reality.

About the author

John Boyne was born in Ireland in 1971. As a child he was always a keen reader. Gripped by stories of adventure and fantasy, he read the whole *Narnia* series in a few days as a twelve-year-old. He always felt that he wanted to be a writer, and he filled notebooks with his short stories and poems.

He studied English at Trinity College in Dublin and later did a creative writing course at the University of East Anglia. After leaving university, he worked in a bookshop in Dublin, getting up at 5.30am every day to dedicate time to his writing before going to work. His first novel, *The Thief of Time*, was published in 2000.

The Boy in the Striped Pyjamas is Boyne's first novel for children. Barely pausing for sleep, Boyne wrote the entire draft in a few days – although there were several drafts before Boyne and his publisher were completely satisfied.

Facts and figures
Published 2006.
It has won two Irish Book Awards and was shortlisted for the British Book Award.
Adapted into a film in 2008.

Chapter 1

Before reading, revise with the children the function of an opening: to hook the reader. Read the chapter and discuss the focus on Bruno. Highlight the social class detail. (Maria's *head bowed* and Mother avoids talking in front of servants.) Examine the writing style, referring to childish labels (*Hopeless Case*), repetition (*causing chaos*) and capital letters (*Out Of Bounds…*). Highlight the conversation about lights. Ask: *During what period is it set?* (War time, with imposed blackouts.) Assess the chapter's success. Have the characters, dialogue and intrigue hooked the reader?

Chapter 2

Read Chapter 2, pausing to contrast the size and atmosphere of the *empty, desolate place* they have moved to with Berlin's *enormous* house and people *strolling along*. Examine the balance of power, commenting on Maria's deferential *Master Bruno*; Father's view of Maria as *overpaid*; the *unhappy* and *angry* waiter; and the *whispering* maids. Consider Bruno's discussion with Maria. Ask: *Why is Bruno afraid of the door's creak?* (He doesn't want someone hearing him criticising Father's job, especially to a servant.) Examine the final paragraph, focusing on the final sentence and how it draws the reader on to the next chapter to discover why Bruno feels *cold and unsafe*.

Chapter 3

Refer to Bruno and Gretel's relationship, commenting that sibling grumbles are light relief after the last chapter's tension. Ask: *Is 'Out-With' a strange name? Which earlier name was strange?* (The Fury.) *Are* nasty *and* unpleasant *objective descriptions of Gretel and her friends?* Point out that things are only presented as Bruno sees them. Investigate the conversation about *other children*. Why is Gretel reluctant to look? (Bruno's demeanour is unnerving.) Draw their attention to the ending, noting that the reader is left wondering.

Chapter 4

Read to where Bruno says *'You see?'* What does Gretel see? (Lots of young and old males.) Focus on the description of outside. Ask: *What details stick in your mind?* (The garden, the bench and the high wire fence.) Continue reading, asking: *What is Gretel's conclusion?* (She assumes it's the countryside.) Read to the end of the chapter. Identify physical reactions: Bruno's need for an *arm around him*; Gretel's *quiet voice*. Is proximity (*not fifty feet*) a factor? Discuss their horror at the sight of dirty children: Bruno's sensitive excuses (*'But maybe they don't have any baths?'*) and Gretel's dismissive incomprehension. Ask: *What does Bruno finally notice?* (The identical clothes.)

Chapter 5

Read Chapter 5 pausing at *Since arriving…* Identify movement back in time with *earlier* and *that morning*. Encourage the children to consider Mother's comment about 'the Fury'. Ask: *Why does Maria unsettle Mother?* (She may have heard her negative comments.) Discuss the overcrowded train, also going eastwards. Finish the chapter and identify the date mentioned: *'forty two*. (Is this date significant?) Ask: *How is Father's room different?* (It is grander.) *What is revealed about Father and Bruno's relationship*? (Father listens to Bruno's concerns but does not take them seriously and demands obedience.)

Chapter 6

Read the chapter. Refer to Maria's entry. Which movement is revealing? (She bows her head to Bruno.) Together, scan Bruno and Maria's dialogue. Ask: *What surprises Maria?* (Bruno regards her as *part of the family*.) *What surprises Bruno?* (Maria is *a person with a life and a history all of her own*.) *What characteristics are revealed about Father?* (His kindness, generosity and sense of duty.) Examine Gretel's entrance and contrast her haughty manner with Bruno's *shouted* defence of Maria. Ask: *What shows Bruno's stress?* (His *overwhelming urge to cry*.)

Guided reading

Chapter 7

Pause after …*just plain nasty* and contrast Bruno's physical coldness with Gretel's reaction to Kotler. Discuss Kotler's treatment of Pavel. Ask: *Why does Bruno look away?* (He is ashamed.) Continue reading, focusing on the fall and rescue. Point out Bruno's initial panic at Pavel being *the only one here* and then bewilderment that a waiter is a doctor. Ask: *What do Pavel's enigmatic words about an astronomer mean?* (People are not everything they seem.) *Why does Mother claim credit?* (She fears trouble.)

Chapter 8

Read the chapter and ask: *What happy memories does Bruno have of Grandmother?* (She loved parties, singing and devising plays.) Encourage the children to explore the events of Christmas Day. Ask: *What leaves Grandmother unimpressed?* (Father's uniform.) *Why does she compare him to a puppet?* (She implies he is being controlled.) Examine the argument's progression and identify important words (*doing the terrible, terrible things you do*). What is Father's defence? (He is a *patriot*.) Do the children understand this term?

Chapter 9

Read up to *But then things changed*. Ask: *What are Bruno's complaints about 'Out-With'?* (He dislikes Gretel's moods, the soldiers and Kotler's overbearing presence.) Consider Kotler's *whispering alone* with Mother. Would Father approve? Continue reading to the end. Discuss Herr Liszt's anger *just waiting to get out, sinister voice* and attitude to learning and *The Fatherland* (Germany). Examine the new information about the striped pyjama people and Bruno's innocent observation that they never come to dinner. Debate his decision to explore. Are they surprised he breaks a rule?

Chapter 10

Read the chapter and comment on the build up

to meeting Shmuel, highlighting the repetition of the words *dot, speck, blob* and *figure*. Next, concentrate on the meeting and ask: *Why does Bruno say* 'We're like twins'? (They share a birth date.) *What makes Bruno change the subject?* ('*We're superior*' sounds wrong and he doesn't want to upset Shmuel.) Compare Bruno's childish babble about being *pushed from pillar to post* with Shmuel's realistic talk of Europe, location and languages. Ask: *Has Shmuel had to grow up?* Emphasise the importance of Bruno's final question and how it compels further reading.

Chapter 11

Look together at the opening and identify time movement in the connective *Some months earlier*. Ask: *What confirms 'the Fury' as incorrect pronunciation?* (Father corrects Bruno.) *What do the preparations and Gretel reveal?* ('The Fury' has power.) Encourage the class to consider Father's instructions to Bruno and Gretel. Ask: *Is it reasonable not to behave* 'like children'? Focus on the arrival of 'the Fury' and his behaviour. What is Bruno's judgement? (He views him as *the rudest guest* and *a horrible man*.) Re-read Mother and Father's argument and establish who wins. (Father as he refuses *to hear another word*.)

Chapter 12

Point out the chapter title's return to the present and the final question in Chapter 10. Read the chapter and ask: *What differences do the boys discover?* (The removal of Shmuel's mother, overcrowding and starvation.) Identify Bruno's innocent reactions such as: suggesting they board his train; exploration; play; incredulity that 11 people shared a room; a dinner invitation. Comment on the cruel contrast of Bruno's roast-beef dinner. Let the children re-read the final page. Ask: *Why is Bruno secretive about the meeting? Does he sense danger?*

Chapter 13

Read up to the end of the boys' conversation.

Guided reading

Ask: *Why is Bruno happier?* (He enjoys meeting Shmuel.) Identify textual evidence of Maria's nervousness (*suspiciously, relieved, froze*). Read on and remark on Mother's attempt to protect Kotler from Father's dinner questions. Ask: *What do the questions imply?* (Kotler's father has avoided fighting.) Encourage the children to consider all of this chapter's events and ask: *Why is the chapter title applied to a short incident?* (It has an important effect on Bruno.)

Chapter 14

Read the chapter and investigate the development of Bruno: his need for Gretel when lacking company and his protective instincts towards Shmuel. Ask: *What characteristics does Bruno show by not blurting out the truth?* (Quick-thinking.) *Is the imaginary friend story useful?* Suggest that it allows Bruno to safely share the secret of Shmuel. *What does Bruno realise about what Shmuel has told him?* (Shmuel is suffering loss and is sad.)

Chapter 15

Examine the causes of Bruno's dislike of Kotler (Mother's and Gretel's reactions; he calls Bruno *little man*; and is *looking around as if this were his house*). Highlight how Mother speaks to him. Is Mother's relationship appropriate? Comment on Bruno's realisation that people from the other side *shouldn't be here in his house*. Why is Shmuel scared to take food? Ask: *Why does Bruno deny knowing Shmuel?* Discuss his cowardice, subsequent shame and Shmuel's forgiveness. Does Shmuel understand the effect of fear? Ask: *What is the final line's effect?* (Touching hands is poignant.)

Chapters 16 and 17

Read about the visit to Berlin. Discuss Mother's realism about 'the Fury's' wreath: *Grandmother would turn in her grave*. Read on, focusing on the siblings' conversation. Ask: *Why is Gretel reading newspapers and moving pins?* (She marks war developments.) Point out confirmation that

Bruno says 'Out-With' incorrectly. Examine the dialogue about the fence. What does Bruno think? (People on his side are kept out.) What does Gretel know? (People on the other side are locked in and excluded.) Identify the casual, shocking acceptance in *'Because they're Jews'*. Ask: *Is the haircut incident funny?* (No, as Bruno's *dwindling self-confidence* implies importance.)

Read Chapter 17 and identify Mother's explicit loneliness (her increased naps and sherries). Analyse the children's conversation with Father. Ask: *What helps Father's decision?* (Bruno mentions the striped pyjamas children.) *Is Father shielding them from reality?*

Chapter 18

Read and identify the incomprehension of Shmuel's life (Bruno justifies Shmuel's Papa's disappearance with *stay there for a few days* and *the post isn't very good*.) Remark on Bruno's embarrassment at expressing his emotions, yet his strong desire for them to play, *Just to remember*. Ask: *How does Bruno first react to Shmuel's idea?* (Doubtfully.) *Are the disguise and haircut persuasive factors?* Encourage comparisons of the boys' *high spirits* about the next day. Ask: *What are their hopes?* (Bruno wants adventure, while Shmuel wants help finding Papa.) Suggest their hopes reflect contrasting lives.

Chapters 19 and 20

Read Chapter 19 and encourage the children to consider what Bruno sees in the camp. What type of place is it? Ask: *What prompts Bruno's decision to leave?* (It might rain.) *What do we learn about Shmuel's hopes?* (He thought the search would fail.)

Explore Chapter 20 and ask: *Why is the first sentence surprising?* (Bruno's story has ended.) *Who suffers most afterwards?* (Father as he realises Bruno's fate.) Identify Father's physical (*legs... stop working*) and mental collapse (*he didn't really mind what they did to him*). Together, re-read the final lines. Does the writer reassure or express uncertainty about history repeating itself?

Shared reading

Extract 1

- Read an enlarged copy of Extract 1 and invite the children to explain where and who Bruno is with. (Father, in his office.)
- Circle the words *this time*, *rude* and *unco-operative*. Ask: *What can you infer?* (Earlier questions may have displeased Father.)
- Underline *'Who are all those people outside?'* Comment on the simple directness: Bruno and the reader await an answer.
- Ask: *Is the question expected?* (No, as Father is *a little confused*.) Examine Father's response, highlighting his delaying tactics: *nodding his head*, *smiling* and repeating *'Those people'*. Circle the ellipsis and discuss what it indicates (hesitation).

- Next, highlight: *they're not people at all; not as we understand the term; nothing whatsoever in common with them*. Suggest the reader's revulsion and compare this to Bruno's confusion in *frowned*, *'They're not?'* and *unsatisfied*.
- Underline *standing up and raising an eyebrow*. What does this silent reminder imply? (Practice and importance.) Read from *He pushed* to the end of the extract, identifying precise movements, formal voice and pronunciation.
- Finally, highlight *'Heil, Hitler'* and comment on the shocking confirmation to the reader. Ask: *What does Bruno's translation reveal?* (A child's innocence.)

Extract 2

- Explain to the class that, here, Bruno's family are having dinner with Lieutenant Kotler.
- Identify Pavel as the waiter. Circle *crashing* and *glug-glug-glugging*. Ask: *Which sense is appealed to?* (Hearing.) *Why is 'glug' repeated and extended?* (It emphasises the spill is extensive.)
- Underline *directly onto the young man's lap* and discuss how suspense is created. (Kotler's previous antipathy towards Pavel warns of a reaction.)
- Read the second paragraph and circle *unexpected*, *extremely unpleasant* and *angry*. How

is brutality implied? (Through the reactions of Bruno's family.)
- Continue reading to the end and highlight comments about Bruno's father (*not even Father – stepped in*; *Father was generally a very kind and thoughtful man*). Ask: *Can Bruno resolve these conflicting thoughts?*
- Focus on Bruno's concerns, highlighting *keep his mouth shut and cause no chaos*. Has the incident changed Bruno? (He is scared of getting into trouble.)

Extract 3

- Read the extract and identify that Bruno and Shmuel are in a crowded room in the camp.
- In the first line circle *it*, referring to the room, and *air-tight*. Ask: *Are there sinister connotations?* (Air cannot enter or gas escape.) *What is Bruno's reaction?* (Highlight *wait here till it* [rain] *eases off*, identifying his trusting naivety.) *Is Shmuel's reaction more realistic?* Contrast how he seems scared, by picking out *gathered himself very close to Bruno* and *in fright*.
- Divide the class into two to read aloud the dialogue. Identify Bruno's childishness,

underlining *play*. Ask: *What indicates developing maturity?* (Bruno expresses compassion by saying *'I'm sorry we didn't find your papa'*.)
- Focus on Shmuel's only spoken words in the extract, underlying *'It's all right'*. Comment on Shmuel's passivity.
- Read the remaining paragraphs and circle the words *gasp* and *metallic*. What is Bruno's innocent explanation? (It stops people catching colds.)
- Finally, highlight and discuss the phrase *nothing in the world would have persuaded him to let it go*. Ask: *Is Bruno's eventual fear exposed?*

Extract 1

Chapter 5: Out Of Bounds At All Times And No Exceptions

Bruno thought about his question, wanting to phrase it exactly right this time, just in case it came out as being rude or unco-operative. 'Who are all those people outside?' he said finally.

Father tilted his head to the left, looking a little confused by the question. 'Soldiers, Bruno,' he said. 'And secretaries. Staff workers. You've seen them all before, of course.'

'No, not them,' said Bruno. 'The people I see from my window. In the huts, in the distance. They're all dressed the same.'

'Ah, those people,' said Father, nodding his head and smiling slightly. 'Those people…well, they're not people at all, Bruno.'

Bruno frowned. 'They're not?' he asked, unsure what Father meant by that.

'Well, at least not as we understand the term,' Father continued. 'But you shouldn't be worrying about them right now. They're nothing to do with you. You have nothing whatsoever in common with them. Just settle into your new home and be good, that's all I ask. Accept the situation in which you find yourself and everything will be so much easier.'

'Yes, Father,' said Bruno, unsatisfied by the response.

He opened the door and Father called him back for a moment, standing up and raising an eyebrow as if he'd forgotten something. Bruno remembered the moment his father made the signal, and said the phrase and imitated him exactly.

He pushed his two feet together and shot his right arm into the air before clicking his two heels together and saying in as deep and clear a voice as possible – as much like Father's as he could manage – the words he said every time he left a soldier's presence.

'Heil, Hitler,' he said, which, he presumed, was another way of saying, 'Well, goodbye for now, have a pleasant afternoon.'

Extract 2

Chapter 13: The Bottle of Wine

But after he had filled Father's glass and turned to refill Lieutenant Kotler's, he lost his grip of the bottle somehow and it fell crashing, glug-glug-glugging its contents out directly onto the young man's lap.

What happened then was both unexpected and extremely unpleasant. Lieutenant Kotler grew very angry with Pavel and no one – not Bruno, not Gretel, not Mother and not even Father – stepped in to stop him doing what he did next, even though none of them could watch. Even though it made Bruno cry and Gretel grow pale.

Later that night, when Bruno went to bed, he thought about all that had happened over dinner. He remembered how kind Pavel had been to him on the afternoon he had made the swing, and how he had stopped his knee from bleeding and been very gentle in the way he administered the green ointment. And while Bruno realized that Father was generally a very kind and thoughtful man, it hardly seemed fair or right that no one had stopped Lieutenant Kotler getting so angry at Pavel, and if that was the kind of thing that went on at Out-With then he'd better not disagree with anyone any more about anything; in fact he would do well to keep his mouth shut and cause no chaos at all. Some people might not like it.

His old life in Berlin seemed like a very distant memory now and he could hardly even remember what Karl, Daniel or Martin looked like, except for the fact that one of them was a ginger.

Text © 2006, John Boyne

Extract 3

Chapter 19: What Happened the Next Day

In fact it felt completely air-tight.

'Well, that's something,' he said, glad to be out of the storm for a few minutes at least. 'I expect we'll have to wait here till it eases off and then I'll get to go home.'

Shmuel gathered himself very close to Bruno and looked up at him in fright.

'I'm sorry we didn't find your papa,' said Bruno.

'It's all right,' said Shmuel.

'And I'm sorry we didn't really get to play, but when you come to Berlin, that's what we'll do. And I'll introduce you to…Oh, what were their names again?' he asked himself, frustrated because they were supposed to be his three best friends for life but they had all vanished from his memory now. He couldn't remember any of their names and he couldn't picture any of their faces.

'Actually,' he said, looking down at Shmuel, 'it doesn't matter whether I do or don't. They're not my best friends any more anyway.' He looked down and did something quite out of character for him: he took hold of Shmuel's tiny hand in his and squeezed it tightly.

'You're my best friend, Shmuel,' he said. 'My best friend for life.'

Shmuel may well have opened his mouth to say something back, but Bruno never heard it because at that moment there was a loud gasp from all the marchers who had filled the room, as the door at the front was suddenly closed and a loud metallic sound rang through from the outside.

Bruno raised an eyebrow, unable to understand the sense of all this, but he assumed that it had something to do with keeping the rain out and stopping people from catching colds.

And then the room went very dark and somehow, despite the chaos that followed, Bruno found that he was still holding Shmuel's hand in his own and nothing in the world would have persuaded him to let it go.

Text © 2006, John Boyne

Plot, character and setting

Understanding the writer

Objective: To read between the lines and find evidence for their interpretation.
What you need: Copies of *The Boy in the Striped Pyjamas*, photocopiable page 15 and writing materials.
Cross-curricular link: History.

What to do
● After reading Chapter 1, explain to the class that, in the opening pages, the writer must accustom the reader to his style. Ask: *Does the writer favour dialogue or narrative description?* (There is a balance.) *How does he treat characters?* (Bruno receives the most attention.)
● Revise the difference between explicit (stated) and implicit (suggested) information. Suggest that the author filters descriptions, opinions and information through Bruno's conversations or thoughts.
● Identify *a Hopeless Case*. Ask: *Is this what the family calls Gretel?* (It is probably just Bruno's opinion.) *Why are capital letters often used?* (To emphasise important words in Bruno's life.)
● Point out Bruno's early questions: '*What's going on? Are we moving?*' What can the reader infer from Mother's resulting actions? (She does not speak in front of the servants, as she does not regard them as equals.)
● Hand out photocopiable page 15 and ask the children to locate the text quoted, explore its context and complete the sections.

Differentiation
For older/more confident learners: Ask the children to locate and write about textual evidence that informs the reader about Gretel, Father or the household.
For younger/less confident learners: Allow the children to work in pairs and focus on examining two of the pieces of textual evidence.

Story journal

Objective: To sustain engagement with longer texts, using different techniques to make the text come alive.
What you need: Copies of *The Boy in the Striped Pyjamas*, photocopiable page 16, journal/exercise books for all, writing materials, internet access to paintings and music (optional).

What to do
● After reading Chapter 1, advise the children that this story has various layers and may be complicated to follow. Suggest using a journal to keep track of the plot developments.
● Discuss what information to include in a journal, such as: events since the last entry; character development; points of interest; dates and places mentioned; unusual language; personal response; and predictions.
● Propose regular journal entries, for example after reading each chapter. Advise following a set format, so that chapters of character development or plot development are obvious.
● Hand out photocopiable page 16 and discuss what to include in the journal entry for Chapter 1. Encourage personal reactions to the novel.
● For the final section, talk about varied media forms. The children may express their response with an illustration or poster, or may use a well-known painting or piece of music.
● Hand out an exercise book and invite the children to write their first journal entry. (Suggest using a double-page spread and the photocopiable sheet as a template.)

Differentiation
For older/more confident learners: Encourage the children to produce longer entries and to identify key quotations and episodes that develop the plot.
For younger/less confident learners: Let the children focus on what has happened and their personal reactions to the story, rather than predicting what might happen.

Plot, character and setting

Character traits

> **Objective:** To appraise a text quickly, deciding on its value, quality or usefulness.
> **What you need:** Copies of *The Boy in the Striped Pyjamas,* photocopiable page 17 and writing materials.
> **Cross-curricular link:** PSHE.

What to do

● After finishing Chapter 6, propose identifying character traits of household members, such as Bruno, Gretel, Father, Mother and Maria.

● Invite the children to scan Chapters 1 and 2 and consider Maria's behaviour. Can they describe her in one adjective? (Respectful or wise.) Ask them to write down their chosen adjective and note textual evidence.

● Let talk-partners share ideas. Do they agree with each other's choice? Choose children to report to the class.

● Display photocopiable page 17 and ask pairs to scan the text as far as the end of Chapter 6 and to consider each character's behaviour. They need to apply appropriate adjectives to describe each of the five characters.

● Provide each pair with a copy of the photocopiable sheet and suggest they aim at four or five adjectives for each character, but advise that some characters may reveal fewer traits.

● Review their answers during a whole-class discussion.

> **Differentiation**
> **For older/more confident learners:** Ask the children to work independently and then read Chapter 7 in order to examine Lieutenant Kotler.
> **For younger/less confident learners:** Assist the children with a bank of adjectives and allow them to concentrate on just three characters.

Marking time

> **Objective:** To locate resources for a specific task, appraising the value and relevance of information and acknowledging sources.
> **What you need:** Copies of *The Boy in the Striped Pyjamas* and writing materials.
> **Cross-curricular link:** History.

What to do

● After reading Chapter 9, ask the children if they remember the date displayed on the bench's plaque. Let them make a note of *June nineteen forty* and its significance: the opening of 'Out-With' camp.

● Are other dates mentioned in the novel? Suggest scanning Chapter 5 and then note the phrase: *since the start of 'forty-two* in the discussion about 'Out-With'.

● Ask: *What time references are made in Chapter 7?* (Bruno remembers a conversation when he was six, *just over three years before they all arrived at Out-With.* Mother said *'War…I'm afraid we'll*

be spending too much time talking about it soon.')

● Return to Chapter 9 and ask: *What does Bruno tell Herr Liszt about his history?* (*I was born on April the fifteenth nineteen thirty-four.*) *How old is Bruno?* (Nine.) *What is the present date in the story?* (It works out to be between April 1943 and April 1944.)

● Ask the children to draw a timeline spanning 1934 to 1945, marking information noted from the story, and the actual beginning and end of the Second World War.

● Review their timelines, checking for accuracy.

> **Differentiation**
> **For older/more confident learners:** Invite the children to work out the chronology of other story incidents and add them to the timeline.
> **For younger/less confident learners:** Encourage partner collaboration and provide page references to help them locate dates and events.

Plot, character and setting

Mapping places

Objective: To read between the lines and find evidence for their interpretation.
What you need: Copies of *The Boy in the Striped Pyjamas* and writing materials.
Cross-curricular link: Geography.

What to do
● After reading Chapter 10, comment on 'Out-With's' central role in the story and express surprise that the author has not supplied a map.
● Remind the children that Boyne uses Bruno's observations and conversations to provide information and suggest that he is doing the same with 'Out-With's' location. (The author expects the reader to interpret textual clues.)
● Ask the children to divide a piece of paper into four squares with the chapter numbers 1, 4, 5 and 10.
● Invite them to scan Chapter 1. Ask: *Where is the family's original house?* (Berlin) *Are they moving far?* (Mother tells Bruno: *It's more than a mile away. Quite a lot more than that.*) Ask them to record findings and evidence about location in the square labelled Chapter 1.
● Next, let them independently search for location evidence in Chapters 4, 5 and 10, making notes in the relevant squares.
● Display a map showing the locations of Berlin and 'Out-With' (Auschwitz in South Poland), asking the children to use their findings to verify that the positions on the map are correct.

Differentiation
For older/more confident learners: Ask the children for a map showing the camp's layout.
For younger/less confident learners: Encourage partner collaboration and supply page references to help them identify evidence.

Causing confusion

Objective: To understand underlying themes, causes and points of view.
What you need: Copies of *The Boy in the Striped Pyjamas,* photocopiable page 18 and writing materials.
Cross-curricular link: PSHE.

What to do
● After completing Chapter 12, suggest that Bruno is constantly confused.
● Direct the children to Chapter 1. Ask: *What puzzles Bruno?* (The need to move.) Also identify confused tension in Chapter 2 when the window view makes him feel *cold and unsafe.*
● Invite them to explore Chapter 5. Why does Bruno think that 'Out-With' cannot be the family home? (*'But Grandfather and Grandmother are in Berlin,' he said. 'And they're our family too. So this can't be our home.'*)
● Next, re-visit Chapter 7. Ask: *Why is Bruno confused by Pavel?* (A waiter claims to be a doctor.)
● Direct the children to Chapter 9 and discuss Bruno's confused reaction to household moods and behaviour, and the presence of soldiers, particularly Kotler. What puzzles Bruno about Mother and Father's dinner guests? (*...they'd never once invited any of the striped pyjama people to dinner.*)
● Provide the children with photocopiable page 18 and direct them to Chapter 12. Explain that when these situations occur, Shmuel and Bruno interpret them differently. Ask the children to complete the sheet, quoting textual evidence to support their answers.

Differentiation
For older/more confident learners: Ask the children to identify and comment on two instances of confused understanding during the meeting in Chapter 10 as well.
For younger/less confident learners: Let the children work in pairs and focus on two of the conversation topics.

Plot, character and setting

Reading moods

Objective: To recognise rhetorical devices used to argue, persuade, mislead and sway the reader.
What you need: Copies of *The Boy in the Striped Pyjamas*, writing materials, individual whiteboards and pens.

What to do

● After finishing Chapter 17, comment that the story's mood has varied considerably in Chapters 13 to 17. Ask the children to scan these chapters and encourage partner discussion. Then invite them to write and hold up three appropriate mood words on their individual whiteboards. Is there some class agreement?

● Invite the children to divide their page into four sections with these mood headings: 'Fear', 'Sadness', 'Tension' and 'Loneliness'. Focus on fear and ask: *When is fear obvious? What words does the writer use? Which words make you also feel this mood?* Encourage partner, and then class, investigation before identifying examples. (For

example: Pavel at dinner; Shmuel's reply when Bruno talks about Kotler; Bruno's reaction to his bald reflection.)

● Encourage the children to write a short paragraph about the mood of fear in these five chapters, quoting textual evidence and commenting on specific language that they find particularly effective.

● Allow time for the children to investigate the five chapters for the other three moods. Remind them to think about the effect the writer wants, and to refer to and quote from the text.

Differentiation
For older/more confident learners: Ensure the children work independently and ask them to explore two further moods, such as sympathy, disappointment and guilt.
For younger/less confident learners: Encourage partner collaboration and ask for writing on only two or three moods.

Confronting reality

Objective: To write reflectively about a text, distinguishing between the attitudes and assumptions of characters and those of the author.
What you need: Copies of *The Boy in the Striped Pyjamas* and writing materials.
Cross-curricular link: History.

What to do

● After finishing the book, emphasise Bruno's confused innocence. Ask: *How does he react to the long room that was surprisingly warm?* (He thinks they are sheltering from the rain.)

● Remind the children that Bruno, the author and the reader are closely linked, as the author uses Bruno's eyes and ears to inform the reader. Explain that the reader is ignorant at first, but gradually becomes knowledgeable by absorbing information, such as: time references (1940s Germany); vocabulary (*Commandant; efficiency; Heil Hitler*); Shmuel's armband; Gretel's

pronouncement about *Jews*.

● Talk about the Holocaust and the Final Solution and their impact on children and adults in Germany and other countries. You may wish to refer to the BBC Primary history website.

● Display and ask the following questions: *Who are the people in the striped pyjamas? Why are they in the camp? What happens to Bruno and Shmuel?*

● Invite the children to write three paragraphs to answer the questions posed and help a young reader face what this novel is about.

Differentiation
For older/more confident learners: Invite the children to add and answer two further questions that they consider important.
For younger/less confident learners: Encourage partner collaboration and allow them to concentrate on answering two of the three questions.

Plot, character and setting

Understanding the writer

- Locate the textual evidence and then write what Bruno thinks and what the author implies.

Textual evidence	What does Bruno think?	What does the author imply?
…his mother had always told him that he was to treat Maria respectfully and not just imitate the way Father spoke to her.		
'Is it further than a mile away?' 'Oh my,' said Mother with a laugh, although it was a strange kind of laugh…		
'Well, I don't like the way we have to turn all the lights off at night now,' he admitted. 'Everyone has to do that,' said Mother. 'It keeps us safe.'		
…he heard her speaking loudly to him until Father spoke louder than Mother could and that put a stop to their conversation.		

Text © 2006, John Boyne

Plot, character and setting

Story journal

● After reading each chapter of the novel, write a journal entry to keep track of the plot.

Date:	Chapter reached:
What has happened since the last entry?	
Character developments:	Atmosphere and attitudes:
Time and place references:	Special vocabulary:
My current reaction to the story so far:	
What I think will happen next?	
My idea for a supporting art form for this section: (Recommend a famous painting or piece of music. Alternatively, add your own artwork on the back of the sheet.)	

SECTION
4

Character traits

● Write down adjectives to describe the character traits displayed in Chapters 1–6. Provide textual evidence to support your answers.

Character	Adjectives	Textual evidence
Bruno		
Gretel		
Father		
Mother		
Maria		

Causing confusion

● There is some confusion when Bruno and Shmuel meet and talk. Explain their separate thoughts about each of the conversation topics below.

Shmuel knows…

Bruno thinks…

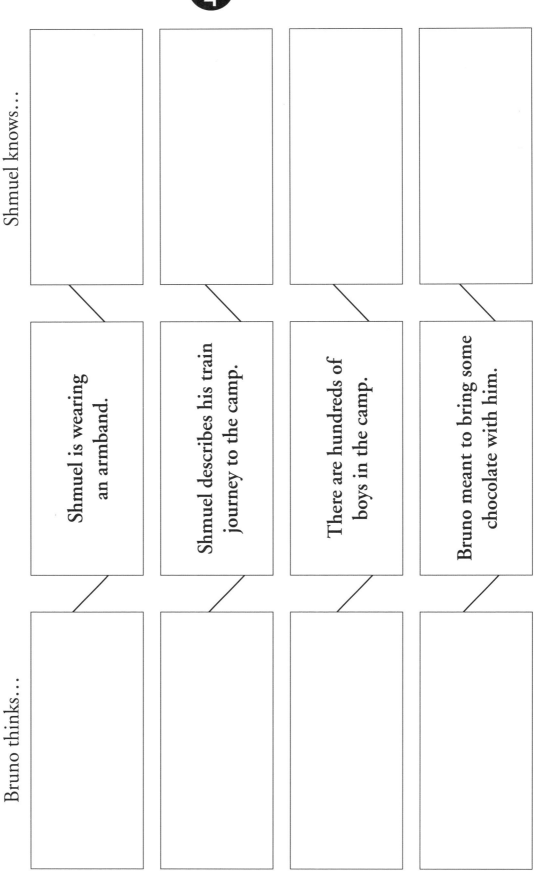

Shmuel is wearing an armband.

Shmuel describes his train journey to the camp.

There are hundreds of boys in the camp.

Bruno meant to bring some chocolate with him.

Talk about it

Adding dialogue

> **Objective:** To work collaboratively to devise and present scripted and unscripted pieces that maintain the attention of an audience, and reflect on and evaluate their own presentations and those of others.
> **What you need:** Copies of *The Boy in the Striped Pyjamas* and writing materials.
> **Cross-curricular link:** Drama.

What to do
● After reading Chapter 3, encourage the children to investigate the dialogue between Gretel and Bruno. Point out that their bickering offers light relief from the tension.
● Direct them to Chapter 1, where Bruno thinks about his friends and their plans. Suggest that, at this point, the author could have effectively slipped back in time to let the reader hear the boys' dialogue.
● Arrange the children into groups of four and highlight the words *'But we had plans'*. Explain that they need to write a playscript in which they supply the missing dialogue as the boys make their plans. Encourage them to become familiar with Bruno's speech style and expressions.
● Provide time for the groups to work on the dialogue. Encourage improvised dialogue before the children write their playscript and stage directions. Remind them to use language and humour to suit Bruno and other nine-year-olds.
● Encourage groups to share and assess other groups' scripted performances.

> **Differentiation**
> **For older/more confident learners:** Ask the children to write the dialogue for a meeting in Berlin between Bruno, his friends, Gretel and her sarcastic friends.
> **For younger/less confident learners:** Allow the children to limit dialogue to two pieces of speech per character and provide them with words or expressions that Bruno could use.

Speaking up

> **Objective:** To tailor the structure, vocabulary and delivery of a talk or presentation so that it is helpfully sequenced and supported by gesture or other visual aid as appropriate.
> **What you need:** Copies of *The Boy in the Striped Pyjamas*, photocopiable page 22 and writing materials.
> **Cross-curricular link:** Drama.

What to do
● Arrange the children into pairs and invite them to scan Chapter 9. Ask: *Why is Bruno uneasy about Kotler?* Identify Kotler's close relationships with Mother and Gretel.
● Discuss the letter in Chapter 8 where Bruno lists things that confuse and sadden him. Re-visit Chapter 7 and ask: *How does Bruno feel about Kotler's insolence to Pavel?* (Ashamed and uncomfortable.) *Why doesn't he intervene?* (Fear.)
● Explain that Bruno has another meeting with Father where he can talk about his concerns/fears. Encourage them to take on the role of Bruno. As speakers, they must organise their thoughts and act out, not just read, their words. Discuss techniques for keeping listeners engaged. (Vocabulary, sequence, gesture and visual aid.)
● Hand out photocopiable page 22 and ask the children to write cue cards. These will be prompts containing brief notes and reminders of techniques to use during the conversation.
● Let them practise in pairs and progress to groups. Encourage listeners to become Father, rating how seriously they take Bruno's worries.

> **Differentiation**
> **For older/more confident learners:** Invite the children to compose Father's response to Bruno.
> **For younger/less confident learners:** Let the children concentrate on writing three cue cards and speak in small groups.

Talk about it

Personal dilemmas

> **Objective:** To improvise using a range of drama strategies and conventions to explore themes such as hopes, fears and desires.
> **What you need:** Copies of *The Boy in the Striped Pyjamas* and writing materials.
> **Cross-curricular link:** PSHE.

What to do

● After reading Chapter 15, comment that the author has made Bruno a good character; nevertheless, fear of being in trouble is a weakness affecting his decisions.

● Tell them to consider the incident in the kitchen when Kotler accuses Shmuel of stealing and Bruno denies knowing Shmuel.

● Divide the class into two groups: Group A to represent Bruno's good side; Group B his bad side. Ask Group A to think of short comments so that Bruno will speak in defence of Shmuel. Then invite Group B to think of remarks to encourage Bruno to deny knowing him.

● Arrange the two groups in facing parallel lines. In role as Bruno, explain that you will walk slowly down the 'alley' between the lines, while the children speak their points. Having listened to 'your conscience' (their voices), make a decision about whether Bruno will help Shmuel.

● Choose children to also play Bruno. Do they reach the same decision?

● Use new conscious alleys for other incidents such as, his claim of an imaginary friend. (Should Bruno tell Gretel?)

> **Differentiation**
> **For older/more confident learners:** Ask the children to plan a conscience alley for Mother after Pavel helps Bruno.
> **For younger/less confident learners:** Allow the children to work in pairs and highlight events to help them focus on why Bruno is scared of Kotler.

Frozen moments

> **Objective:** To consider the overall impact of a live or recorded performance, identifying dramatic ways of conveying characters' ideas and building tension.
> **What you need:** Copies of *The Boy in the Striped Pyjamas*, photocopiable page 23 and writing materials.
> **Cross-curricular link:** Drama.

What to do

● Pause after finishing Chapter 15. Suggest to the class that photographs of the story's tense moments would reveal the characters' feelings. Explain the term 'freeze-frame', in which children create a silent tableau of characters at a moment in the story.

● Arrange the children into groups of six. Provide each group with a card from photocopiable page 23 to act out. Encourage collaborative decision-making to allocate roles, consult text and rehearse a freeze-frame.

● Invite each group to present their freeze-frame to the class. Does the audience recognise the moment? Let individuals step out of the tableau and speak their character's thoughts.

● For other characters use thought-tracking, by inviting a member of the audience to stand next to a frozen character and speak their thoughts. Ask: *How can you know what to say?* (Characters' facial expressions and body language.)

● Finish with the groups exchanging cards and repeating the activity, this time with more expressive facial expressions and body language.

> **Differentiation**
> **For older/more confident learners:** Ask the children to adapt their freeze-frame, departing from the story or changing a character's personality or reaction. Can they explain their alterations?
> **For younger/less confident learners:** Help the children to analyse their chosen character's thoughts and reactions, modelling movements and expressions.

Talk about it

Father figure

> **Objective:** To participate in whole-class debate, using the conventions of debate, including standard English.
> **What you need:** Copies of *The Boy in the Striped Pyjamas*, photocopiable page 24 and writing materials.
> **Cross-curricular link:** Citizenship.

What to do

● After completing the book, focus on the character of Father. Briefly discuss his role in the novel and write some of his character traits on the whiteboard (such as a sense of duty, a belief in rules, ambition and pride).

● Explain to the children that they are going to examine the character of Bruno's father and prepare an oral case to determine if he is good or bad.

● In preparation for the class debate, hand out photocopiable page 24 and ask the children to examine Father's actions, deciding whether they are good or bad deeds. A list has been provided, but encourage them to find their own points. The completed sheets should help them compose convincing points, using textual evidence.

● Once their notes are complete, divide the class into two groups, assigning them the task of either arguing that Father is good or bad.

● Chair the debate formally, listening to the arguments and ensuring everyone contributes.

● Finally, sum up the arguments. Encourage the children to listen carefully to help them decide if Father is good or bad. Give them a 'free' vote as individuals, not as members of one side.

> **Differentiation**
> **For older/more confident learners:** Ask the children to prepare a similar case for or against Mother. Is she weak or strong?
> **For younger/less confident learners:** Allow the children work in pairs and provide page references to help them develop the lists of deeds.

Making decisions

> **Objective:** To use exploratory, hypothetical and speculative talk as a tool for clarifying ideas.
> **What you need:** Copies of *The Boy in the Striped Pyjamas* and writing materials.
> **Cross-curricular link:** PSHE.

What to do

● After completing the book, suggest that minor plot decisions may have a large impact. Re-visit Chapter 11 and Father's announcement about dinner with 'the Fury'. Put the children into pairs, with one acting as Mother and one as Father. Pose the hypothetical question: *What if Mother keeps her theatre arrangements?* (Father may not become Commandant.) On your signal, let partners improvise dialogue for two minutes.

● Stop the improvisations, but leave one pair in character for others to question about their feelings and decisions.

● Invite the pairs to repeat the exercise with Bruno and Father's meeting in Chapter 5, exchanging the role of Father. Ask: *What if Father becomes worried about Bruno?* (They may return to Berlin.) Again, hot-seat a new pair.

● Continue with conversation about *an imaginary friend* in Chapter 14. Ask: *What if Bruno admits the truth?* (Gretel may inform her parents.)

● Finally, improvise the scene in Chapter 19, asking: *What if Bruno refuses Shmuel's plea to search?* (Bruno may return home safely.)

● As a class review their work. What decisions are made? Is Bruno's fate changed?

> **Differentiation**
> **For older/more confident learners:** Encourage the children to pose questions for meetings between Bruno and Maria.
> **For younger/less confident learners:** Provide the children with useful conversation openers, such as: 'I love the theatre…'; 'I think "the Fury" is…'

Talk about it

Speaking up

● Imagine you are Bruno preparing to speak to Father about your experiences and concerns at 'Out-With'. Cut out the cue cards and make notes to use during your conversation.

The truth about Pavel: What did he do for you? What is his job? Speaking technique:	**Lieutenant Kotler's behaviour:** How does he treat Pavel? How did you feel? Speaking technique:
Lieutenant Kotler's presence: Why is he around so much? Does he have a good effect on Gretel? Speaking technique:	**The wire fence:** Why is it there? Do you understand what is beyond it? Speaking technique:
The low huts and smoke stacks: Do you think they look pleasant? Do you understand their purpose? Speaking technique:	**Making suggestions:** Where do you want to live? Speaking technique:

Frozen moments

● Cut out the cards and create freeze-frames of these key events from *The Boy in the Striped Pyjamas.*

✄

Freeze-frame 1 'The Fury' and Eva have come to dinner. Father has introduced Bruno and Gretel. Mother looks anxious. Bruno shakes hands with 'the Fury' and Gretel wobbles as she curtseys.	**Freeze-frame 2** Mother, Gretel and Bruno sit with plenty of space, comfortably on a train. Bruno sees another train across the tracks, where people are squashed together. Both trains are travelling eastwards.
Freeze-frame 3 Lieutenant Kotler is having dinner with the family. Pavel is waiting on them but the bottle of wine slips from his fingers. The wine empties onto Kotler's lap.	**Freeze-frame 4** From upstairs, Bruno watches and listens. Father, at his office doorway, talks to soldiers in uniform, their caps under their arms. They praise Father's appointment to 'Out-With'.
Freeze-frame 5 Lieutenant Kotler is having dinner with the family. Pavel is standing by the wall. Father is asking Kotler why his father left Germany for Switzerland.	**Freeze-frame 6** In the kitchen, Kotler has asked Bruno if he knows Shmuel. In other rooms, Mother drinks a sherry, Gretel moves pins on a map and Maria, with her eyes downwards, puts clothes away.

Talk about it

SECTION 5

Father figure

● Analyse the character of Bruno's father by considering his actions and decide if they are good or bad. A few examples have been added for you.

Good points	Bad points
Father pays for Maria's mother's hospital care.	Father questions why Lieutenant Kotler's father moved to Switzerland.

● You may wish to categorise the list of actions listed below, but also try to add your own findings from the novel.

Father pays for the funeral of Maria's mother.
Father teaches the children the importance of good behaviour.
Father follows 'the Fury's' commands.
Father insists that 'the Fury' must come to dinner.
Father introduces Bruno and Gretel to 'the Fury'.

Get writing

Effective language

> **Objective:** To experiment with the visual and sound effects of language, including the use of imagery, alliteration, rhythm and rhyme.
> **What you need:** Copies of *The Boy in the Striped Pyjamas* and writing materials.
> **Cross-curricular link:** Art and design.

What to do

● After reading Chapter 4, comment that the writer often links meaning and the sounds of the words used to convey atmosphere, mood and attitude, particularly Bruno's.

● Ask the children to re-read the second paragraph of Chapter 2 and contrast the writing styles. For example, the light, happy language and idealised descriptions for Berlin's house (*a quiet street, other big houses, always nice to look at*) against the harsh, extreme tone for the new house (*all on its own in an empty, desolate place… no other houses anywhere*).

● Next, encourage them to analyse the description of Berlin's streets. Highlight the alliteration (*strolling* and *stopping, cabbages, carrots, cauliflowers and corn*), imagery (*feeling his head grow dizzy with the mixed scents of sweetness and life*) and rhythm in balanced lists of pairs of foods (*leeks and mushrooms, turnips and sprouts*).

● Suggest that Bruno pictures school in Berlin as equally attractive. Ask the children to imagine Bruno's school and write a description, using alliteration, imagery, rhythm and rhyme to emphasise the happy sense of place.

● Allow them to share ideas with a partner and make preliminary drafts.

> **Differentiation**
> **For older/more confident learners:** Encourage the children to write a similar description of Bruno's kitchen in Berlin.
> **For younger/less confident learners:** Allow the children to collaborate and to just focus on using alliteration and imagery.

Involving the reader

> **Objective:** To use a range of narrative devices to involve the reader.
> **What you need:** Copies of *The Boy in the Striped Pyjamas*, photocopiable page 28 and writing materials.
> **Cross-curricular link:** History.

What to do

● After reading Chapter 8, revise first and third person writing. Direct the children to the book's first page and the pronouns *he, she* and *him*, making it third person.

● Point out that the writer shows an empathy with Bruno through his focus on him. Nevertheless, there are ways the author could involve himself and the reader more closely.

● As a class, discuss narrative devices that will further involve the author and reader. Talk about: asides from the author; brackets to divide the story from the asides; the use of the pronouns *I* for the author and *you* for the reader; comparisons between the novel's historical context and the author/reader's own time.

● Hand out photocopiable page 28 and explain to the children that they need to take on the role of the author and provide the reader with four commentary pieces for significant parts of the story. In order to avoid confusion, these should be written in the first person (*I*) and the reader to be addressed as *you*.

● Review their work, checking for appropriate language, style and placement in the book.

> **Differentiation**
> **For older/more confident learners:** Ask the children to research rail travel, eastwards from Berlin, in 1943 and use the information in a commentary.
> **For younger/less confident learners:** Allow the children to focus on writing two commentaries.

Get writing

Story planning

> **Objective:** To independently write and present a text with the reader and purpose in mind.
> **What you need:** Copies of *The Boy in the Striped Pyjamas*, photocopiable page 29 and writing materials.
> **Cross-curricular link:** History.

What to do

● Invite the class to imagine that Boyne is to write a sequel in keeping with the original book. Ask: *What could stay the same?* (Perhaps the same family, another innocent main character, the writing style or the historical period.) *What could change?* (There could possibly be new characters, plotline or another difficult issue.)
● Invite partners to share ideas for a new book. Prompt them with questions and possible answers, such as: *When is the story set?* (1944.) *What is the difficult issue?* (The bombing of Berlin.) *Who is the innocent character?* (Gretel.) *What does she do?* (She helps an injured pilot.) *What is the ending?*

(She is made homeless.)
● Discuss other possible Second World War issues, for example: enemy collaboration; refugees; punishment and retribution; physical and psychological trauma.
● Recap with the class a story's structure of chronological sections (opening, incidents, complications, resolution and ending). Talk about the value of subplots and character development to hold the reader's attention.
● Provide the children with photocopiable page 29 and invite them to create a story plan. Keep the plans for the next lesson activity.

> **Differentiation**
> **For older/ more confident learners:** Encourage the children to develop detailed character notes.
> **For younger/less confident learners:** Allow the children to work in pairs and concentrate on the incidents and resolution (avoiding the complications and dilemmas).

Becoming writers

> **Objective:** To set their own challenges to extend achievement and experience in writing.
> **What you need:** Completed story planners from 'Story planning' activity, copies of *The Boy in the Striped Pyjamas* and writing materials.
> **Cross-curricular link:** History.

What to do

● Remind the children of the previous lesson activity (planning a sequel to *The Boy in the Striped Pyjamas*).
● Re-read Chapter 4, which is typical of Boyne's style of writing, and emphasise that they need to match it when writing. Highlight the paragraph lengths, detailed descriptions, abundant dialogue and the application of direct speech rules. Comment on innocent vocabulary, childish simplicity (*higher even than the house they were standing in,*) and emphasised spoken words (*nine, I, is*). Do they let the reader 'hear' the speakers?

● Point to the final sentence in Chapter 4 and comment that Boyne often finishes chapters with confusion, bewilderment or reader anticipation.
● Return the children's 'Story planning' sheets from the previous session. Let them recap their plans by telling their story outline to a partner.
● Allocate time for the children to write their story, and suggest they consider a target length and add it to their notes.
● Allow the children to write their story. Once complete, review their work together.

> **Differentiation**
> **For older/ more confident learners:** Invite the children to utilise literary devices, such as similes, metaphors and onomatopoeia in their writing.
> **For younger/less confident learners:** Encourage the children to work in groups of up to five and share the writing, each developing one section of the story.

Get writing

Expressing a view

> **Objective:** To establish, balance and maintain viewpoints in non-narrative texts.
> **What you need:** Copies of *The Boy in the Striped Pyjamas* and writing materials.
> **Cross-curricular link:** Citizenship.

What to do

● After completing the novel, tell the children that 27 January is Holocaust Memorial Day. Explain it is a time to remember the people who were murdered, mostly Jews, by the Nazis in the Second World War. Suggest that in this novel, especially its final, explicit three sentences, Boyne makes a significant contribution to this day.

● Comment that teachers may have mixed views about choosing this novel for their Year 6 class. Hold discussions in favour of using it, considering: historical knowledge; the need to know what mankind is capable of; it being a warning against the repetition of genocide. Move on to talk about the disadvantages, for example: it is a distressing subject; there could be confusion between history and fiction; the brutal reality and tragic ending.

● Explain that school magazines help teachers make book selections. Suggest that a popular magazine is writing an editorial about this novel. Show the class an editorial, pointing out features including: clear standpoint, arguments, reasons, evidence, statistics and quotes. Emphasise that an editorial attempts to persuade readers to have the same view.

● Ask the children to plan and write an editorial about *The Boy in the Striped Pyjamas*.

> **Differentiation**
> **For older/more confident learners:** Ask the children to write a second editorial, taking the opposing view.
> **For younger/less confident learners:** To help the children structure their editorial, provide a writing frame, signalling the introduction, arguments, reasons and summary.

Cover design

> **Objective:** To use varied structures to shape and organise text coherently.
> **What you need:** Copies of *The Boy in the Striped Pyjamas*, photocopiable page 30 and writing materials.
> **Cross-curricular link:** Art and design.

What to do

● Explain to the class that some books are published in two editions, with one for adults and one for children. Discuss examples by authors such as, JK Rowling and Philip Pullman. Emphasise that these 'crossover' books appeal to adults and children.

● Point out that, in crossover novels, the two editions differ in their cover design: the front-cover illustration and the back-cover blurb (information) and quoted reviews. Show the children some example covers.

● Suggest that *The Boy in the Striped Pyjamas* is a crossover novel. Then explain to the children that they need to imagine they are working with the publisher to agree on a new front and back cover for the children's edition.

● Arrange the children into pairs to discuss covers. Help them by asking: *How much information will you supply? How can you advise people about whether the book will suit them? Will the cover have universal appeal? Which newspapers and magazines will you quote reviews from?*

● Hand out photocopiable page 30 and invite the children to design their covers.

> **Differentiation**
> **For older/more confident learners:** Ask the children to also design the new book cover for the adult edition.
> **For younger/less confident learners:** Invite the children to work in pairs and just focus on designing the front cover, adding one review quote.

Get writing

Involving the reader

● Imagine you are the author, write four commentaries to involve the reader more closely with the story. Decide where in the novel to place them.

Place between Chapters __ and __	Place between Chapters __ and __
Place between Chapters __ and __	Place between Chapters __ and __

Story planning

● Use the planning frame below to help you develop a sequel to *The Boy in the Striped Pyjamas*.

Opening (Where? When? Who?)
Incidents (What are the disturbing events? What is the innocent development?)
Complications and dilemmas (Who has a difficult decision to make? What do they decide? What goes wrong?)
Resolution (Is the confusion cleared up? Is a wrong decision made?)
Ending (What is the final result? Is it happy or sad?)

Cover design

● Design a new front and back cover for the children's edition of *The Boy in the Striped Pyjamas.*

● What effect do you hope your words and picture will have?

Assessment

Assessment advice

Confusion and tension run through *The Boy in the Striped Pyjamas*. Demonstrate this by arranging the class into pairs as Bruno and Gretel, and encouraging them to discuss in improvised dialogue what they see from the window. Listen for confusion and observe tense body and facial language. Use a similar paired activity to assess the class awareness of Bruno and Shmuel's different emotional states and confused understanding of each other's lives.

Father's decisions control the plot, so allow the children to consider his position by acting out, in pairs, a disagreement between Father and Mother. Expect recognition that Father imposes his job's consequences on the family. You might also decide to take the hot-seat as Grandmother, answering the children's questions about the Christmas argument. What do they think

Grandmother opposes and why is she ashamed of her son?

Difference and division are important themes in the novel. Create a 'fence' in the classroom to represent the divided world in the story. Place half the class on each side, asking them to act as if they live there. From the children's demeanour and actions, assess their awareness of freedom and a sense of superiority on one side, captivity and misery on the other. Also assess the children's understanding of the different childhoods Bruno and Shmuel experience by placing them in pairs to take on either role. As they walk to and from one of their meetings, do they display Bruno's excited play and Shmuel's sad, weak movements? Ask them about what they eat. Do the children know that Bruno will eat plenty, while Shmuel will starve?

Knowing the truth

> **Objective:** To understand underlying themes, causes and points of view.
> **What you need:** Copies of *The Boy in the Striped Pyjamas*, photocopiable page 32 and writing materials.

What to do
● Explain to the class that this story is fictional, but it is set within historical reality. In the novel, the author focuses on Bruno, presenting people, places and things through this child's innocent interpretation. By the end of the book, with Bruno gone, the facts behind the story are evident.
● Hand out photocopiable page 32 and ask the children to work individually to explain what the reader understands after completing the novel. This activity will allow you to check the children's recognition of the facts beyond the fiction and to assess their ability to deduce implicit information.

● Depending on the children's research and history work, expect the following sorts of answers:

● **'The Fury'**: Adolf Hitler, addressed as 'Fuhrer' Leader of the Nazi Party and Germany.
● **'Out-With'**: Auschwitz is a concentration camp in Poland, where mainly Jewish refugees were killed by the Nazis.
● **Pavel**: A camp member who is made to be a waiter. He is Jewish, so forbidden to be a doctor.
● **Father**: His uniform signifies his job is Commandant of Auschwitz. On his armband is a swastika, the Nazi Party's symbol.
● **The striped pyjamas**: Everyone in the camp is forced to wear this uniform, which makes escape impossible.
● **The march and air-tight room**: This is when camp inmates were rounded up, herded into the gas chamber and killed.

Knowing the truth

● After completing the novel explain the factual truth that the reader understands about the following.

Father: What does his uniform reveal? What is his job? What is on his armband?

The striped pyjamas: Why do all the people in the camp wear them?

The march and air-tight room: Why are there marches? What happens in the room?

'The Fury': Who is he? What is his title? Why is he powerful?

'Out-With': What is the place really called? Where is it? Who lives there?

Pavel: Who is he? Is he being greedy and taking two jobs?

■SCHOLASTIC
www.scholastic.co.uk